STEPHEN J. NICHOLS

What Is The Christian
Faith All About?

CF4•K
Because you're never
too young to know Jesus

Copyright © 2024 Stephen J. Nichols

Hardback ISBN: 978-1-5271-1138-7
E-book ISBN: 978-1-5271-1204-9

10 9 8 7 6 5 4 3 2 1

Published in 2024
by
Christian Focus Publications,
Geanies House, Fearn, Tain, Ross-shire,
IV20 1TW, U.K.
www.christianfocus.com

Cover and internal design by
Francisco Adolfo Hernández Aceves

Printed and bound by Gutenberg, Malta

CONTENTS

I am so grateful for Stephen's book, *Bible Basics*! He is such a skilled scholar who can communicate in an accessible way to youth; which isn't easy! I wish I would have had this book when I was growing up, but am so glad to put this into the hands of my own children and students. Such a helpful volume!

John Perritt
Director of Resources for Reformed
Youth Ministries; host of The Local Youth
Worker podcast, author; father of five

Reading the Bible can be daunting, especially if you are unfamiliar with its contents. The apostle Paul exhorted the Corinthian church, "do not be children in your thinking" (1 Cor. 14:20) and *Bible Basics* is what you need to fulfill Paul's exhortation. Packed with information, Dr. Nichols takes you on a whirlwind tour from Genesis to Revelation pointing the landmarks along the way. A perfect beginner's guide to understanding the Bible.

Derek W. H. Thomas
Chancellor's Professor, Reformed
Theological Seminary
Teaching Fellow, Ligonier Ministries

With brevity and clarity, Stephen Nichols lays a solid foundation for the new student of God's Word to help jumpstart a lifetime of study and growth. Like wise words from a tour guide when visiting a new city, *Bible Basics* orients the reader to the twists and turns, highlights and landmarks of the most important book ever written. This is a resource I wish I had as a new teenage convert and one that my four children will be reading. *Bible Basics* is a gift to the church and a new generation of believers.

Nathan W. Bingham
Vice President of Ministry Engagement and Executive
Producer and Host of Renewing Your Mind,
Ligonier Ministries

INTRODUCTION:
BACK TO THE BASICS

The movie *Hoosiers* retells the story of the "Milan Miracle," when the coach of a small-town Indiana, U.S.A., high school basketball team accomplished the impossible. In 1954, the Milan High School, with a total enrollment of merely 161 students, won the state championship. However, when the season started, in the movie version at least, the team was far from championship material. What did the coach do? He started with the fundamentals. Fundamentals are the foundational principles, or the primary and central principles. Another word for the fundamentals is *the basics*. The coach went back to the basics. He allowed no shooting baskets and held no scrimmages in those early practices. It was running, dribbling, passing. Repeat. Repeat again. The basics came first, and the basics had to be mastered. Then came the games, then came victories, and then came the state championship.

This book offers some Bible basics as the foundation for discipleship and doctrine. Here you will find an overview of the biblical books, places, and events. We'll look at the big picture of the Bible by exploring the idea of the covenant. You'll find some key biblical passages to meditate upon and memorize, as well as prayers from the Bible. You'll also find key ideas from the centuries of church history. Together we'll walk through basic doctrines in order to have a better grasp on what the Bible teaches. You'll even find some hymns.

These basics provide a foundation upon which to build a solid faith. In fact, all of us, no matter where we find ourselves in our Christian walk, need these fundamentals. We need to go back to the basics. Repeat. Repeat again.

The Reformer Martin Luther once declared, "Though I am a great doctor, I have not yet progressed beyond the instruction of children in the Ten Commandments, the Apostles' Creed, and the Lord's Prayer. I still learn and pray these every day with my Hans and my little Lena."

Luther was telling us that the basics matter. We all need to master these basics of the Bible. Let's get started.

THE BOOKS OF
THE BIBLE

The word *Bible* comes from the Greek word, *Biblion,* meaning book. The Bible is one book made up of sixty-six books. Around AD 200, the church father Tertullian first referred to the collection of thirty-nine books as "The Old Covenant" or "The Old Testament." The Jews referred to these thirty-nine books as "The Law," "The Prophets," and "The Writings," referring to how they organized and grouped these books together. These books span a millennium, from the time Moses wrote the Pentateuch in the fifteenth century BC through the 400s BC.

Cannon Vs. Canon

Cannon with two "N"s goes boom! It shoots cannon balls to avoid.

Canon with one "N" does not go boom. It is the rule of faith and life we run into—not away from!

Tertullian, The Church Father

Tertullian lived around AD 160-220. In addition to coining the terms Old and New Testaments, he also coined the very important word, "Trinity." We call the leaders in the early church the Church Fathers because they helped the church grow in its early years and in the establishment of the historic Christian faith. The era of the Church Fathers spans from AD 100 – 400.

Tertullian also coined the term "New Testament." The New Testament consists of twenty-seven books all written in the first century AD. Most of these books are epistles or letters, a very common genre in first-century Rome. The New Testament also consists of books of history and a book of prophecy.

God divinely inspired the human authors of Scripture (2 Peter 1:16-21). These sixty-six books constitute the canon of Scripture. The word canon means "a reed" or "a measuring rod." The idea is of a standard or rule. The canon of Scripture is the rule or the measure for doctrine and life. Canon also refers to the standard or the criterion by which these books are considered divinely authored and, consequently, authoritative texts.

A book is in the canon of Scripture based on four criteria. First, it directly claims to be the word of God. Take for instance the Old Testament prophetic books with the refrain, "Thus says the Lord." Secondly, the content of the book is in keeping with the content of the other books. The teaching of the book is in harmony with the overall teaching of the Bible. Thirdly, the author is a prophet or apostle, or uniquely associated with a prophet or apostle and is called by God to write His word. Lastly, the book has wide acceptance and recognition. It doesn't simply represent a small group or one location.

We need to realize one more thing regarding the canon, Protestants believe the church recognizes these sixty-six books as the canon by seeing the book reflect these criteria. The key word here is recognize, as the church does not determines or establishes the book as part of the biblical canon.

The Bible = 66 Books

The Old Testament = 39 Books

The New Testament = 27 Books

BIBLE BASICS

The Books of The Old Testament

Genesis	1 Chronicles	Daniel
Exodus	2 Chronicles	Hosea
Leviticus	Ezra	Joel
Numbers	Nehemiah	Amos
Deuteronomy	Esther	Obadiah
Joshua	Job	Jonah
Judges	Psalms	Micah
Ruth	Proverbs	Nahum
1 Samuel	Ecclesiastes	Habakkuk
2 Samuel	Song of Solomon	Zephaniah
1 Kings	Isaiah	Haggai
2 Kings	Jeremiah	Zechariah
	Lamentations	Malachi
	Ezekiel	

The Books of New Testament

Matthew	Ephesians	Hebrews
Mark	Philippians	James
Luke	Colossians	1 Peter
John	I Thessalonians	2 Peter
Acts	2 Thessalonians	1 John
Romans	1 Timothy	2 John
1 Corinthians	2 Timothy	3 John
2 Corinthians	Titus	Jude
Galatians	Philemon	Revelation

Who Wrote the Bible?

The Bible is a book from God to us. In giving us the Bible, God used human authors to write the various books that comprise the Bible. God used highly educated authors like Moses, who had the very best education of the day in Pharoah's house. God also used authors like Peter, a fisherman, who would have likely had a minimal education. God worked through the styles and personalities of these biblical authors. Every word of the Bible and all of the words of the Bible are true because every word and all the words come from God. Who were the different human authors? As for the Old Testament authors, we'll start with Moses.

Moses	Author of Genesis, Exodus, Leviticus, Numbers, and Deuteronomy, and also Psalm 90
Ezra	Author of 1 & 2 Chronicles and Ezra
Nehemiah	Author of Nehemiah
Solomon	Author of Proverbs (with others), Ecclesiastes, and Song of Songs
Isaiah	Author of Isaiah
Jeremiah	Author of Jeremiah and Lamentations
Ezekiel	Author of Ezekiel
Daniel	Author of Daniel
Hosea	Author of Hosea
Joel	Author of Joel
Amos	Author of Amos
Obadiah	Author of Obadiah
Jonah	Author of Jonah

Micah	Author of Micah
Nahum	Author of Nahum
Habakkuk	Author of Habakkuk
Zephaniah	Author of Zephaniah
Haggai	Author of Haggai
Zechariah	Author of Zechariah
Malachi	Author of Malachi

David wrote most of the Psalms, but other authors contributed. They include:

Asaph	Moses
Ethan	Solomon
Heman	The Sons of Korah

Some of the Psalms were written by anonymous people—we don't know who wrote fifty of the Psalms. The other anonymous books of the Old Testament include:

Joshua	Ruth	Esther
Judges	1 & 2 Samuel	Job
	1 & 2 Kings	

As for New Testament authors, we start with Matthew.

Matthew	Author of Matthew
John Mark	Author of Mark
Luke	Author of Luke and Acts
John	Author of John, 1, 2, and 3 John, and Revelation

Paul	Author of Romans, 1 & 2 Corinthians, Galatians, Ephesians, Philippians, Colossians, 1 & 2 Thessalonians, 1 & 2 Timothy, Titus, and Philemon
James	Author of James
Peter	Author of 1 & 2 Peter
Jude	Author of Jude

There is one anonymous book in the New Testament, the book of Hebrews.

The Genres of the Old Testament

The word genre refers to a category of writing or literature. The Old Testament includes books of law, narratives and histories, poetry, and prophecy. The Hebrew Bible offers three major groupings for the thirty-nine books: the Law, the Writings, and the Prophets. Jesus, following this custom, used these designations when he referred to the Old Testament.

Law	Writings	Prophets
Torah	Ketuvim	Nevi'im

The Law specifically refers to the first five books of the Bible. These books contain historical narratives, poetry, and laws and treaties. The events of the Pentateuch span from the very first day of history on through the period known as the Ancient Near Eastern World. The word Pentateuch comes from two Greek words. *Penta* means five and *Teuchos* means scroll or book. The Pentateuch is the first five books of the Bible. Jews refer to these books as the Torah, from the Hebrew word that means "law." As governments today write laws, so did governments back then. Also, nations would enter into treaties or covenants with other nations in Old Testament times. Consequently, we find the language of laws and of covenants or treaties throughout these five books. For an example of laws, see Exodus 20. For an example of a covenant, see the covenant God made with Abraham in Genesis 12:1-3.

Law   Genesis
Exodus
Leviticus
Numbers
Deuteronomy

Jews refer to the Writings as the *Ketuvim*, the Hebrew word for *writings*. These books consist of two main genres, history (or narrative) and poetry. The historical books use the narrative genre form. In narrative, you have three main elements. You have the setting, you have the characters, and you have the plot. Look at Exodus 3. What's the setting? Who are the characters? Now, what's the plot or the development of the story?

Most English poetry uses rhyme. Hebrew poetry rhymes thoughts or ideas. The big word we use here is *parallelism*. There are different types of parallelism. The author can say the same thing twice to make a point. Or, the author can say two opposite things to make a contrast. Another feature of Hebrew poetry is to use as few words as possible, keeping it short and sweet.

Can you find the parallel words in Psalm 100:4?

Enter his gates with thanksgiving,
and his courts with praise.

Writings

History	Poetry
Joshua	Job
Judges	Psalms
1 & 2 Samuel	Proverbs
1 & 2 Kings	Ecclesiastes
1 & 2 Chronicles	Song of Solomon
Ezra	
Nehemiah	
Esther	

The Jews refer to the Old Testament prophetic books as the *Nevi'im*. *Nevi* is the Hebrew word meaning *prophet*, and *nevi'im* is the plural meaning *prophets*. The prophetic books have the genres of poetry, history, and even law and covenant. They also contain, as their name has it, prophecy. Prophecy uses vivid metaphors and colorful descriptions to paint a picture of things to come. Sometimes we also use the word *apocalyptic* to describe the genre of prophecy. Look at Ezekiel Chapter 1 and you'll see his imagery of four living creatures, a wheel, and a

The Tanakh

Jews refer to the Hebrew Bible as the *Tanakh*. This is made up of words for the three divisions of the law, prophets, and writings.

Torah
+ Nevi'im
+ Ketuvim
= TaNaKH

wheel within a wheel. The prophets are divided into the major prophets, which are longer books, and the minor prophets, which are shorter.

Prophets

Major	Minor
Isaiah	Hosea
Jeremiah	Joel
Lamentations	Amos
Ezekiel	Obadiah
Daniel	Jonah
	Micah
	Nahum
	Habakkuk
	Zephaniah
	Haggai
	Zachariah
	Malachi

The Genres of the New Testament

The New Testament consists of three major genres: history, epistles, and prophecy. We've already seen the genres of history and prophecy. The new genre in the New Testament is epistles, or letters. Epistles were a very important form of communication in the first century.

History
Epistles
Prophecy

As in the Old Testament, there is a lot of history in the New Testament. Do you want to try to find the setting, characters, and plot again? Look for all three in John 6:16-21.

History   Matthew
            Mark
            Luke
            John
            Acts

As mentioned, a very popular genre in Greco-Roman times was epistles, or letters. Paul mastered the art of the epistle. Look at the short book of Philemon. In verses 1-3, Paul begins by identifying himself as the author and greets the recipient of the letter, Philemon. Paul concludes the letter in verses 17-25. In between is the body of the letter, which contains the main points Paul wants to teach Philemon.

Greco-Roman Period

This period refers to the times of the Greek Empire and the Roman Empire. It spans from the 300s BC until AD 400.

Paul's not the only one to write letters. James, John, Jude, Peter, and the author of the Epistle to the Hebrews all wrote letters. We classify the New Testament Epistles as Pauline Epistles, those written by Paul, and as General Epistles, the letters written by the others.

Epistles

Paul

Romans	Colossians
1 & 2 Corinthians	1 & 2 Thessalonians
Galatians	1 & 2 Timothy
Ephesians	Titus
Philippians	Philemon

General

Hebrews	1, 2, & 3 John
James	Jude
1 & 2 Peter	Revelation

The final book in the New Testament and in the Bible is in the genre of prophecy or apocalyptic literature. Apocalypse in the Greek language means to lift the cover off, or to reveal. John, who wrote Revelation, received a vision of what is to come. The cover has been lifted. God has revealed His plan for now and eternity. Read Revelation 22:1-5 for a very encouraging vision of things to come.

Prophecy   Revelation

THE BIG PICTURE OF
THE BIBLE

Have you ever tried to put together a puzzle without the picture on the box? The pieces are fascinating, but it's almost impossible to make sense of the pieces without the picture. So it is with the Bible. We tend to look at texts, at individual passages. Occasionally, we look at whole biblical books. But we will be greatly helped if we look at the picture on the box.

The big picture of the Bible is actually quite simple. The Bible is God's story. It is the story of God creating and redeeming a people for Himself and restoring His people to full and glorious fellowship with Him. Ultimately, the Bible declares the glory of God from its first word to its last.

We can see this story as taking part in four movements. Keeping this big picture in mind will help you make sense of all the pieces of Scripture.

Creation

This spans from Genesis 1-2. God created Adam and Eve and placed them in the perfect setting, the Garden of Eden. He provided everything they needed. In the cool of the evening, God came and walked with Adam and Eve; He had fellowship with His creatures. God gave Adam and Eve one command: not to eat of the tree of the knowledge of good and evil.

Fall

This spans from Genesis 3 onwards. Adam and Eve did not keep that one command. They broke the command and suffered the consequences. They were expelled from the Garden and the curse would be the new reality. Every human being is fallen. We are all "in Adam." The fall extends beyond us and even reaches to the very ground. We live in a fallen world. Dietrich Bonhoeffer called it a "fallen-falling world."

Redemption

Even as God was pronouncing the curse in Genesis 3, He was giving the promise of a Deliverer and a Redeemer. This Redeemer would be the Seed to come. It would take millennia, but the Seed would eventually come—as a baby lying in a manger. Jesus Christ did what Adam did not do: He kept the law. Jesus also undid what Adam did: He paid the penalty for transgression and sin. All of those who are redeemed are "in Christ." We still live in a fallen world, however.

The Old Testament points toward Christ. The New Testament Gospels display the work of Christ and proclaim the words of Christ. The New Testament Epistles unpack the meaning of the words and significance of the work of Christ as our Redeemer. While the fall and sin bounce all around and ricochet through human history, Christ and the cross tower over human history.

Restoration

At the fall, Adam and Eve, and all of us along with them, were kicked out of the Garden of Eden. Revelation 21 declares that there will be a new heaven and new earth. We will be restored to the Garden. The curse will be removed and all sin, sorrow, sickness. and sadness, will be removed forever. We will worship God and reign with Him and behold His Glory forever and ever. All things will be made new.

Putting It All Together

When you read the first two chapters of the Bible, you learn about creation. The fall comes in Genesis 3, as does the promise of Christ. If you skip all the way to the end and the final chapters of the book of Revelation, you learn about the restoration and the new heaven and the new earth. In between we learn more about the creation—and what it means to be created in the image of God. We learn about the fall and about all of the ugliness of sin and its effects on us and on this world. We learn about heaven and the future and about the new age to come. And, at the center of it all we learn about Christ and God's plan of redemption.

Enjoy the "puzzle pieces" of biblical passages and verses. As you do, keep in mind the picture on the box and this grand story of Creation, Fall, Redemption, and Restoration.

THE COVENANT

The story of redemption also shines through in the Bible's teaching on the covenant. In fact, the Bible may be seen as one grand covenant. A covenant is an agreement between two parties. The two parties are God and us. Sometimes we also use the word testament as a synonym for the word covenant. The idea of a covenant also includes the idea of promises. These covenants are promises made by God. All of God's promises ultimately point to Christ. Christ is the ultimate fulfillment of the covenants and of God's promises. The beginning of Isaiah 51:15 and the ending of Isaiah 51:16 sum up the covenant:

I am the LORD your God ... You are my people.

We are God's people, "the sheep of His pasture" (Psalm 100:3). God loves His sheep, God cares for His sheep, and God will be faithful in keeping His sheep. We call this one covenant that spans all of Scripture and includes all God's people, the *Covenant of Grace*. This covenant unfolds in a progressive manner through the Bible. This unfolding of the Covenant of Grace comes in the forms of the different biblical covenants.

The biblical covenants are:

The Covenant with Adam and Eve
Genesis 3
The Covenant with Noah
Genesis 9
The Covenant with Abraham
Genesis 12-17
The Covenant with Moses
Exodus 19-24 | Deuteronomy
The Covenant with David
2 Samuel 7
The New Covenant
Jeremiah 31 | Ezekiel 33

Jesus offered Himself as the fulfillment and the apex of the covenant when He instituted the Lord's Supper the night He was betrayed (Matthew 26:26-29). Because Paul preached "Christ and Him Crucified," Paul refers to himself as a minister of the New Covenant (2 Corinthians 3:7-11). Also read Hebrews Chapter 8 to see how Christ fulfills the covenant.

When we study the covenant of grace and the biblical covenants we learn that God always keeps His promises.

ROMANS AND THE GOSPEL

Paul's Epistle to the Romans lays out a clear and extensive discussion of the gospel. The gospel is from a Greek word, *evangelion*. That word means *good news*. Before we can hear the good news, we need to hear the bad news. The bad news is that we are lost and dead in sin and under the wrath of God. The good news is that we can have peace with God.

Romans 1	?	Romans 5
Under the Wrath of God		Peace with God

How do we go from being under the wrath of God to being at peace with God? The answer is the righteousness of God. But, wait. How can we achieve the righteousness of God? We can't. We are sinful and unrighteous. We are the opposite of God's standard of holiness and purity. But there is good news. That good news is the gospel. Jesus, who is perfect and sinless, achieved the righteousness of God through his life of obedience and keeping the law and through his death and paying the penalty for our breaking of the law. The righteousness of God is in Jesus Christ. Romans 1 speaks of the wrath of God. Romans 5 speaks of peace with God. Right in the middle, Romans 3, we learn that we pass from wrath to peace through faith in Jesus Christ. Here's what Paul says in Romans 3:21-26 about Jesus and the good news of the gospel.

> But now the righteousness of God has been manifested apart from the law, although the Law and the Prophets bear witness to it—the righteousness of God through faith in Jesus Christ for all who believe. For there is no distinction: for all have sinned and fall short of the glory of God, and are justified by his grace as a gift, through the redemption that is in Christ Jesus, whom God put forward as a propitiation by his blood, to be received by faith. This was to show God's righteousness, because in his divine forbearance he had passed over former sins. It was to show his righteousness at the present time, so that he might be just and the justifier of the one who has faith in Jesus.

We move from being under God's wrath to peace with God and under His love only through the person and work of Christ.

Romans 1	Romans 3	Romans 5
	The Rigtheousness	
The Wrath of God	of God in Christ	Peace with God

The Romans Road

These key passages from Romans also provide a way to understand the gospel. The Romans Road can also be used as a way to tell others about the gospel.

Romans 1:20-21
Romans 3:10, 23
Romans 5:8
Romans 6:23
Romans 10:9-10
Romans 10:13

Paul further explains the gospel in Romans 5:12-21 by contrasting what it means to be "in Adam" with what it means to be "in Christ". This contrast between being in Adam or in Christ runs deep and wide through Scripture. Here's a summary of the biblical teaching.

IN ADAM	IN CHRIST
Sin	Salvation
Death	Life
Eternal Death	Eternal Life
Condemnation— Judged and found guilty!	Justification— Declared righteous!
Alienation— Separated from God	Reconciliation— United with God
Slavery	Redemption
Bondage	Freedom
Guilt & Shame	Forgiveness
Wrath	Peace

Through the sixty-six books of the Bible and especially here in Romans, these three basic ideas get emphasized again and again:

1. God is holy and totally righteous.
2. We are separated from God because of our sin.
3. We need a substitute who can pay the penalty for our sin and bring us home to God—we need Jesus.

Adam and Eve's sin resulted in a wide gulf between them and God. This gulf is like the Grand Canyon but way, way bigger. Nothing they could ever do would bridge that gulf. God's holiness demands that not even the slightest sin can stand in His presence. We need a substitute, a sacrifice. We see the promise of all this in Genesis 3:15. We likely see the first sacrifice in Genesis 3:21. We certainly see it in the book of Exodus and Leviticus as God gives the instructions for the tabernacle and for the sacrifices.

The word *tabernacle* means *to dwell*. God desires to dwell with His people, but our sin separates us from Him. The sacrifices served as a temporary substitute. When the people of God settled in Israel, Solomon built a temple in Jerusalem (1 Kings 6). The tabernacle was a tent and was portable. As Israel wandered and moved, the tabernacle went with them. The temple was made of stone. It didn't move. Instead, the Israelites living throughout the twelve tribes came to it.

Even though the temple was made of stone, it was not permanent. When Israel was taken captive by Nebuchadnezzar, the temple was destroyed. Under

Nehemiah and Ezra, the temple was rebuilt. But that temple was not permanent, either. It would also be destroyed by the Romans in AD 70.

During His earthly ministry, Christ taught, "Destroy this temple, and in three days I will raise it up" (John 2:19). He was referring to His death, the three days in the tomb, and the resurrection. Jesus is the permanent temple. He is also the permanent sacrifice.

The sacrifices in the Old Testament had to be repeated daily. The Day of Atonement, when the spotless lamb was slain and the blood was sprinkled upon the altar, had to be repeated every year. But not so for the sacrifice Jesus made of His own blood. Jesus made His sacrifice once for all (Hebrews 8-10). It was done once and for all and never needs to be repeated. Jesus' sacrifice is permanent. When John the Baptist first saw Jesus, he declared,

"Behold, the Lamb of God, who takes away the sin of the world" (John 1:29).

That is the good news of the gospel.

What Happens Next?

After salvation comes transformation. God's grace transforms our lives as we conform our lives to God's Word and to the example of Christ—which is all done by the Holy Spirit at work in us. Paul explains transformation as a "renewal of our minds" that is demonstrated in our obedience. He writes of this in Romans 12:1-2:

I appeal to you therefore, brothers, by the mercies of God, to present your bodies as a living sacrifice, holy and acceptable to God, which is your spiritual worship. Do not be conformed to this world, but be transformed by the renewal of your mind, that by testing you may discern what is the will of God, what is good and acceptable and perfect.

After grace comes growth. God's grace given to us at salvation makes us new creatures. We turn from our old ways and turn towards new ways and our new life in Christ. We grow as Christians when we read and obey God's Word. We grow when we pray and seek God's guidance and help in our lives. We grow when we love and serve our neighbors and friends.

Grace $\longrightarrow$ Growth

BIBLICAL EVENTS

It is important to know the events and stories of the Bible. This chart helps us keep the major events in order so that we can walk through the history of the Bible. These events remind us that the Bible took place in space and time, that the Bible records true events of real people in real places.

The Events of the Old Testament

The Pentateuch

Creation: Adam & Eve
Fall
Flood: Noah
Call of Abraham and the Age of the
    Patriarchs, Isaac and Jacob

The Twelve Tribes, Genesis 49

Reuben
Simeon
Levi
Judah
Issachar
Zebulun
Dan
Naphtali
Gad
Asher
Joseph (Later becomes the two tribes of Ephraim & Manasseh)
Benjamin

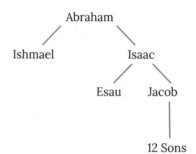

Twelve Sons, Twelve Tribes

Joshua	Slavery in Egypt
	Moses & The Exodus
	Wilderness Wanderings
	Joshua & The Conquest

| Judges | Judges, from Othniel to Samuel |

Historical Books & The Prophets	Kings & Prophets: Saul, David, Solomon
	Divided Kingdom: Judah (Two Southern Tribes) and Israel (Ten Northern Tribes)
	Assyrian Captivity of Israel

Babylonian Captivity of Judah
Exile
Return and Rebuilding
400 Silent Years

The Events of the New Testament

The Gospels

Birth of Christ
Earthly Ministry of
    Christ
Calling of the
    Twelve Disciples
The Final Week,
Palm Sunday
    through Good
    Friday
Crucifixion
Resurrection

Acts

Ascension
Pentecost
Peter's Preaching
Conversion of Paul
Paul's Missionary
    Journeys
Paul's
    Imprisonments
    in Rome

Pentecost

This refers to the Feast of Pentecost. The word means "Fifty," and refers to a feast held fifty days after the Feast of the Passover.

Martyr

The word martyr means witness. Many Christians in the early church, through the centuries, and in our own day have given their lives as a witness to Jesus Christ in times of persecution.

Epistles

Martyrdoms of Paul and Peter
Exile of John to the Island of Patmos

BIBLICAL PLACES

The events recorded in the Bible occurred in both time and space. The Old Testament took place in the Ancient Near Eastern world and the New Testament occurred in the Greco-Roman world.

Babylon, Assyria, Egypt, Medo-Persia—these were the empires and places that serve as the setting for the Old Testament. The ancient civilizations grew along rivers. The Tigris and the Euphrates served Babylon and the great Nile River was the setting for Egypt. As these empires fought and traded, the land of Israel played a key role. Placed right between the eastern Mediterranean coast and the Jordan River, Israel was a significant route. Abraham was called out form Ur of the Chaldees (later Babylon) to the Promised Land. Famine sent the sons of Jacob to Egypt, where they joined their brother, Joseph, whom they had cast into a pit and then sold. The nation Israel became an enslaved people while in Egypt, until God called Moses to deliver His people. After the plagues and the exodus, Israel wandered in the wilderness of the Sinai Peninsula for a generation, before re-entering the promised land.

Israel was bordered to the West by the Mediterranean Sea and the East by the Sea of Galilee, which flows into the Jordan River and then empties into the Dead Sea—the place of the lowest elevation on the face of the earth at 1,300 feet below sea level.

After Solomon, the kingdom was divided into the Northern and Southern tribes. Assyria took the Northern tribes captive in 733 BC. Babylon took the Southern tribes captive in 597 BC. A generation later, the captives were permitted to return by Cyrus and began rebuilding the city walls of Jerusalem and the temple.

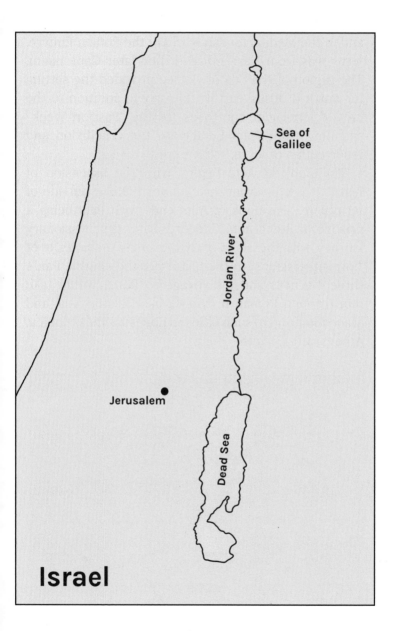

Sea of
Galilee

Jordan River

Jerusalem

Dead Sea

Israel

The New Testament takes place in the land of Israel and in the Mediterranean world of the Roman Empire. Jesus was from Nazareth and then later Capernaum. The region of the Sea of Galilee provided the setting for much of Jesus' earthly ministry in addition to the city of Jerusalem, the focus for the "Passion Week," spanning from Palm Sunday to the crucifixion and resurrection of Jesus.

The Book of Acts begins with the ascension of Jesus to heaven from the Mount of Olives outside of Jerusalem. The Book of Acts ends with Paul being a prisoner in Rome. Acts 13 records Paul's first missionary journey, with the island of Cyprus being the first site of "foreign missions" in the history of the church. Paul's three journeys and his voyage to Rome would take him through Roman provinces like Galatia, Asia, and Macedonia and to such cities as Ephesus, Thessalonica, Athens, and Corinth.

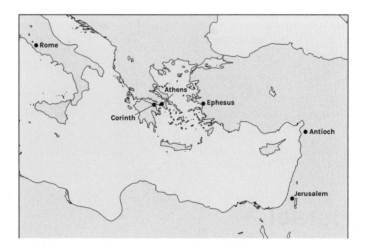

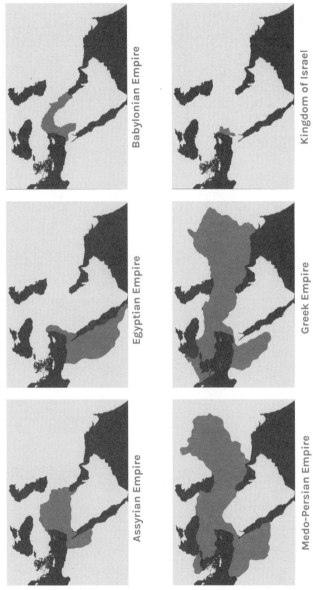

BIBLE MEMORIZATION

Memorizing Scripture is a staple of being a faithful disciple. David memorized and meditated upon the Law of God, upon the first five books of the Bible. When Jesus was tempted in the wilderness, he responded to Satan by quoting Scripture.

Committing Scripture to memory is a discipline that well repays the effort. Here's a very short one to help you get started:

1 Thessalonians 5:17

Pray without ceasing.

And one more short one:

Colossians 3:15b

Be thankful.

Now consider adding these verses to your memory:

Genesis 1:1

> In the beginning, God created the heavens and the
> earth.

Psalm 89:1

> I will sing of the steadfast love of the LORD forever;
> with my mouth I will make known your
> faithfulness to all generations.

Proverbs 3:5-6

> Trust in the LORD with all your heart, and do not
> lean on your own understanding.
> In all your ways acknowledge him, and he will
> make straight your paths.

John 3:16

> For God so loved the world, that he gave his only
> Son, that whoever believes in him should not
> perish but have eternal life.

John 15:12

> This is my commandment, that you love one
> another as I have loved you.

Romans 3:23

> For all have sinned and fall short of the glory
> of God.

Ephesians 2:8-10

> For by grace you have been saved through faith.
> And this is not your own doing; it is the gift of
> God, not a result of works, so that no one may
> boast. For we are his workmanship, created
> in Christ Jesus for good works, which God
> prepared beforehand, that we should walk
> in them.

Psalm 1

> Blessed is the man who walks not in the counsel of
> the wicked,
> nor stands in the way of sinners,
> nor sits in the seat of scoffers;
> but his delight is in the law of the LORD,
> and on his law he meditates day and night.

> He is like a tree
> planted by streams of water
> that yields its fruit in its season,
> and its leaf does not wither.
> In all that he does, he prospers.

> The wicked are not so,
> but are like chaff that the wind drives away.

Therefore the wicked will not stand in the judgment,
    nor sinners in the congregation of the righteous;
    for the Lord knows the way of the righteous,
    but the way of the wicked will perish.

Psalm 23

The Lord is my shepherd; I shall not want.
    He makes me lie down in green pastures.

He leads me beside still waters.
    He restores my soul.

He leads me in paths of righteousness
    for his name's sake.

Even though I walk through the valley of the
    shadow of death,
    I will fear no evil,
    for you are with me;
    your rod and your staff,
    they comfort me.

You prepare a table before me
    in the presence of my enemies;
    you anoint my head with oil;
    my cup overflows.

Surely goodness and mercy shall follow me
    all the days of my life,
    and I shall dwell in the house of the
    Lord forever.

THE LORD'S PRAYER & BIBLICAL PRAYERS

When the disciples asked Jesus to teach them to pray, He gave them the answer in the form of the prayer below. Each line, or petition, of this prayer provides a gateway into a broad and expansive horizon. We should note that the Lord's Prayer starts with God. Too often we can't see past our own self, and much of the content of our prayers can be rather self-focused. The Lord's Prayer reminds us of the necessity of the God-focused and God-centered life.

Our Father, who art in heaven,
Hallowed be thy Name.

Thy Kingdom come,
Thy will be done,
on earth as it is in heaven.

Give us this day our daily bread
And forgive us our debts,
as we forgive our debtors.

And lead us not into temptation,
but deliver us from evil.

For thine is the kingdom,
and the power, and the glory,

Forever. Amen.

In addition to the Lord's Prayer, the Bible records many prayers of God's people. Here is a sample of three prayers. Nehemiah's prayer is a prayer of petition and intercession, in which he makes a specific request of the Lord. Mary's "Magnificat" is a prayer of praise and adoration. Finally, Paul lets the Ephesian believers know how he prays for them. As we read these biblical prayers, as well as others, we can learn how to pray in a way that honors God.

Nehemiah's Prayer, Nehemiah 1:4-11

As soon as I heard these words I sat down and wept and mourned for days, and I continued fasting and praying before the God of heaven. And I said,

O LORD God of heaven, the great and awesome God who keeps covenant and steadfast love with those who love him and keep his commandments, let your ear be attentive and your eyes open, to hear the prayer of your servant that I now pray before you day and night for the people of Israel your servants, confessing the sins of the people of Israel, which we have sinned against you. Even I and my father's house have sinned. We have acted very corruptly against you and have not kept the commandments, the statutes, and the rules that you commanded your servant Moses. Remember the word that you commanded your servant Moses, saying, 'If you are unfaithful, I will scatter you among the peoples, but if you return to me and keep my commandments and do them, though your outcasts are in the uttermost parts of heaven, from there I will gather them and bring them to the place that I have chosen, to make my name dwell there.' They are your servants and your people, whom you have redeemed by your great power and by your strong hand. O Lord, let your ear be attentive to the prayer of your servant, and to the prayer of your servants who delight to fear your name, and give success to your servant today, and grant him mercy in the sight of this man.

Mary's Magnificat, Luke 1:46-55

And Mary said,
My soul magnifies the Lord,
and my spirit rejoices in God my Savior,
for he has looked on the humble estate
of his servant.

For behold, from now on all generations will call
me blessed;
for he who is mighty has done great things for me,
and holy is his name.
And his mercy is for those who fear him
from generation to generation.
He has shown strength with his arm;
he has scattered the proud in the thoughts of their
hearts;
he has brought down the mighty from their thrones
and exalted those of humble estate;
he has filled the hungry with good things,
and the rich he has sent away empty.
He has helped his servant Israel,
in remembrance of his mercy,
as he spoke to our fathers,
to Abraham and to his offspring forever.

Paul's Prayer in Ephesians, Ephesians 3:14-19

For this reason I bow my knees before the Father,
from whom every family in heaven and on earth
is named, that according to the riches of his glory
he may grant you to be strengthened with power
through his Spirit in your inner being, so that
Christ may dwell in your hearts through faith—that
you, being rooted and grounded in love, may have
strength to comprehend with all the saints what is
the breadth and length and height and depth,and to
know the love of Christ that surpasses knowledge,
that you may be filled with all the fullness of God.

THE TEN COMMANDMENTS & THE GREAT COMMANDMENT

How should we then live? The Bible has much to say about the topic of ethics, or about our behavior. One of the fascinating things we sometimes overlook about the Ten Commandments is that these commands and ethical demands are given after we are reminded of God's act of redemption. Paul takes a similar approach in his Epistles. He reminds us of who we are in Christ, then he puts our ethical obligations before us. The Ten Commandments are followed by the summary of the New Commandment given by Jesus in the Gospels.

The Ten Commandments
Exodus 20:1-17

I am the LORD your God,
who brought you out of the land of Egypt,
out of the house of slavery:

1. You shall have no other gods before me.
2. You shall not make for yourself an idol.
3. You shall not take the name of the LORD your God in vain.
4. Remember the Sabbath day to keep it holy.
5. Honor your father and mother.
6. You shall not murder.
7. You shall not commit adultery.
8. You shall not steal.
9. You shall not bear false witness against your neighbor.
10. You shall not covet.

The Great Commandment
Matthew 22:34-40

But when the Pharisees heard that he had silenced the Sadducees, they gathered together. And one of them, a lawyer, asked him a question to test him.

"Teacher, which is the great commandment in the Law?"

And He said to him:

"You shall love the Lord your God with all your heart and with all your soul and with all your mind. This is the great and first commandment. And a second is like it: You shall love your neighbor as yourself. On these two commandments depend all the Law and the Prophets."

BIBLICAL WISDOM

The first chapter of 2 Chronicles records a fascinating story. God appears to Solomon and says to him, "Ask what I shall give you." If God were to say to you, "Ask for anything and I will give it to you," what would you ask for? What do you think Solomon asked for? If you said wisdom, you're right.

Wisdom means skillful living. We all need wisdom. Solomon was most wise in asking for wisdom. And God gave it to him. People from all over came to Solomon for his help to solve problems. He was the wisest man. The Old Testament Book of Proverbs contains much of Solomon's wisdom. Proverbs only represents part of the wisdom literature of the Bible. We also need to include Ecclesiastes, Song of Songs, and some of the Psalms. The New Testament Epistle of James may also be considered wisdom literature.

Here are three things you need to know about the Bible's teaching on wisdom. First, wisdom, even all knowledge and learning, begins with the fear of the Lord.

Proverbs 1:7 makes it clear:

"The fear of the LORD is the beginning of knowledge."

To fear God means to honor and revere God as God. It means to acknowledge that God is over everything, that God is the source of everything, and that God is the goal of everything. To fear God means to know that He is pure, holy, perfect, just, true, all-powerful, and eternal. God is the beginning and the end. The life of wisdom begins with the fear of God. Remember to honor God in all things. That is the first thing we need to know about the Bible's teaching on wisdom.

The second thing you need to know concerns the two paths. Read Psalm 1. Do you see the two paths? The one who follows God's Word will be "blessed." That word means happy or fulfilled. It means true joy and contentment. Who does not want that? Do you see the other path? Disobeying God's Word leads to misery, death, and judgment. The Book of Proverbs contrasts the way of the wise with the way of the fool.

The third thing you need to know about the Bible's teaching on wisdom is that it relates to all areas of your life. The wisdom literature of the Bible reaches into every corner. It speaks to work and how we spend our time. It tells us how to relate to our family and friends and neighbors. It tells us how to use our tongue and to watch what we say. It talks about wealth and poverty, kings and servants. Remember, wisdom means skillful living. The Bible's teaching on wisdom aims at that target of living skillfully, obediently, and faithfully.

The Fear of the Lord	Path of Obedience	Blessed/Happy	Skillful Living
Trust in Our Self or Trust in this World	Path of Disobedience	Misery	Folly & Ruin

A Proverb a Day

The Book of Proverbs has thirty-one chapters. You could read a verse from each chapter, or a few verses, or the entire chapter every day of the month.

Proverbs 3:5-7

> Trust in the LORD with all your heart,
> and do not lean on your own understanding.
> In all your ways acknowledge him,
> and he will make straight your paths.
> Be not wise in your own eyes;
> fear the LORD, and turn away from evil.

And ... pray for wisdom. James 1:5 tells us:

> If any of you lacks wisdom, let him ask God, who gives generously to all without reproach, and it will be given him.

Solomon asked God for wisdom and God gave it to him. God invites us to ask for wisdom. And a wise boy or girl, or a wise man or woman, will do just that.

11

RICHES FROM
CHURCH HISTORY

The Bible is our sure foundation and guide. God has also been instructing His church through the centuries. Over those centuries many texts have been helpful summaries of the Bible's teaching or have served as helpful aids in discipleship. Here follows a very brief sampling of some of these riches from our past.

The Apostles' Creed has its roots in the early years of the second century AD in the various bishop's creeds. Over the centuries, these creeds took on a standard form. When we read or say these words, we are joining with the church of the past two thousand years. It's called the *Apostles' Creed* because it summarizes the teaching of the Apostles. The Latin word *Credo* means "I believe." A creed is a belief or a statement of beliefs.

The Apostles' Creed

I believe in God the Father Almighty,
    Maker of heaven and earth.

And in Jesus Christ, his only Son, our Lord,
    Who was conceived by the Holy Spirit,
    and born of the virgin Mary.
    He suffered under Pontius Pilate,
    was crucified, died, and was buried;
    He descended into hell.
    The third day He rose again from the dead.
    He ascended into heaven
    and is seated at the right hand of God the
    Father Almighty.
    From there He will come to judge the living and
    the dead.

I believe in the Holy Ghost,
    the holy catholic church,
    the communion of saints,
    the forgiveness of sins,
    the resurrection of the body,
    and the life everlasting.

                    Amen.

Another creed from the early church comes from the Nicene Council in 325. The false teachings that Jesus was either not truly human or not truly divine were taught in the church. The Nicene Creed affirms the biblical teaching that Jesus is truly human and truly divine. Jesus is the God-man *"for us and for our salvation."* The Creed was re-affirmed at the Council of Constantinople in 381.

Nicea

Nicea was an ancient town in the modern day nation of Turkey. Constantine, the Roman Emperor at that time had a palace in Nicea and invited the church leaders there to have the Nicene Council in AD 325.

The Nicene Creed
325, 381

We believe in one God, the Father
 Almighty, Maker of heaven and
 earth, and of all things visible
 and invisible.

And in one Lord Jesus Christ, the
 only-begotten Son of God,
 begotten of the Father before
 all worlds; God of God, Light
 of Light, very God of very God;
 begotten, not made, being of
 one substance with the Father,
 by whom all things were made.

Who, for us men for our salvation,
 came down from heaven, and
 was incarnate by the Holy
 Spirit of the virgin Mary,
 and was made man; and was
 crucified also for us under
 Pontius Pilate;

He suffered and was buried; and the
third day He rose again, according
to the Scriptures; and ascended
into heaven, and sits on the right
hand of the Father; and He shall
come again, with glory, to judge
the quick and the dead; whose
kingdom shall have no end.

And we believe in the Holy Ghost,
the Lord and Giver of Life; who
proceeds from the Father and
the Son; who with the Father and
the Son together is worshipped
and glorified; who spoke by the
prophets.

And we believe in one holy catholic
and apostolic Church. we
acknowledge one baptism for the
remission of sins; and we look for
the resurrection of the dead, and
the life of the world to come.

Amen.

The Heidelberg Catechism represents one of the key
texts of the Reformation. It was written primarily by
Zacharias Ursinus and Caspar Olevianus at the request of
Elector Frederick III. It was first recited in the Cathedral
of the Holy Spirit in the city of Heidelberg, Germany.

The Heidelberg Catechism 1&2
1563

1   Q. What is your only comfort in life and in death?

A. That I am not my own, but belong—body and soul, in life and in death—to my faithful Savior, Jesus Christ. He has fully paid for all my sins with his precious blood, and has set me free from the tyranny of the devil. He also watches over me in such a way that not a hair can fall from my head without the will of my Father in heaven; in fact, all things must work together for my salvation.

Because I belong to him, Christ, by his Holy Spirit, assures me of eternal life and makes me wholeheartedly willing and ready from now on to live for him.

2   Q. What must you know to live and die in the joy of this comfort?

A. Three things: first, how great my sin and misery are; second, how I am set free from all my sins and misery; third, how I am to thank God for such deliverance.

From 1643–1653, an assembly of over 100 ministers and theologians met in Westminster Abbey and wrote the Westminster Standards, consisting of:

Important Confessions in the Reformed Church

Presbyterian

- The Westminster Standards

Dutch Reformed

- "The Three Forms of Unity"

- The Belgic Confession of Faith

- The Heidelberg Catechism

- The Canons of the Synod of Dordt

Reformed Baptist

- The London Baptist Confession, 1689

The Lutheran Church

- The Augsburg Confession of Faith

The Anglican Church

- The Thirty-Nine Articles

- The Westminster Confession of Faith (WCOF)
- The Westminster Larger Catechism (WLC)
- The Westminster Shorter Catechism (WSC)

The Westminster Shorter Catechism 1 - 3, 1648

1 Q. What is the chief end of man?

   A. Man's chief end is to glorify God, and to enjoy him forever.

2 Q. What rule hath God given to direct us how we may glorify and enjoy him?

   A. The Word of God, which is contained in the Scriptures of the Old and New Testaments, is the only rule to direct us how we may glorify and enjoy him.

3 Q. What do the Scriptures principally teach?

   A. The Scriptures principally teach what man is to believe concerning God, and what duty God requires of man.

The Five Reformation Solas
The 16th Century

The *Solas* summarize the teachings of the Reformers. *Sola* is Latin for *alone*. The "alone" part is the crucial feature. It's not simply that Scripture is our authority; it's that Scripture alone is our authority, and so on with the other *solas*. The *solas* have become a helpful construct to understand the main contribution of the Reformation to our understanding of the Bible, the gospel, and doctrine.

Sola Scriptura
Scripture Alone: The Word of God is the sole authority for the church and for the Christian. The Reformers were careful not to dismiss tradition, while at the same time recognizing that tradition is not authoritative.

Sola Fide
Faith Alone: Salvation is by faith alone apart from works. Faith is a gift from God. We are justified by Christ's work alone. Our sin is imputed to Christ; Christ's righteousness is imputed to us.

Sola Gratia
Grace Alone: Salvation is by grace alone apart from any merits of my own. We need to understand two words: mercy and grace. Mercy is not getting what we do deserve. We deserve punishment for our sins, but God gives mercy to those who trust in Christ. Grace is getting the riches of God we don't deserve. God pours out his grace upon us abundantly and freely when he saves us in Christ.

Solus Christus

Christ Alone: Salvation is found in Christ alone. He is the only way, and He is the only means of salvation.

Soli Deo Gloria

The Glory of God Alone: Salvation ultimately serves to bring glory to God. By stressing that salvation is by grace alone, through faith alone, in Christ alone, the Reformers were emphasizing how salvation leaves no room for us to boast or to brag. A biblical doctrine of salvation reserves all the glory, all the bragging and boasting, for God alone. Salvation is God's work for His glory.

Also, all of life is to be lived for the glory of God alone. This also relates to the Reformer's emphasis on vocation. The Reformers held that all of our work and the different roles we play can all be directed and driven towards glorifying God.

If you ever visit the city of Geneva in Switzerland, you will see the following motto in various places around the old city. It speaks of the light of the gospel shining brightly and piercing the darkness after centuries of the church's decline and the church's neglect of the gospel. The light of the gospel breaks through the darkness.

The Motto of the Reformation at Geneva

Post Tenebras Lux

After Darkness Light

BASIC BELIEFS:
AN INTRODUCTION
TO DOCTRINE

The word *doctrine* comes from the Latin word meaning *to teach*. Doctrine is a belief or a set of beliefs. We sometimes speak of *orthodox* doctrine. *Ortho* means *straight* or *right*. When we say a doctrine is *orthodox* we are claiming that it aligns with God's Word, that it reflects the teaching of the Bible. Over the centuries, different churches have disagreed over certain doctrines or teachings. At the same time, there has been a consistent vein of orthodox teaching concerning the basic beliefs. Orthodox teaching is firstly true to Scripture and is spelled out and presented in the creeds of the early church and the Reformation confessions.

The next few pages contain a basic outline of key doctrines. The church has always seen doctrine as essential to church life and practice. Doctrine is

Key Words

Orthodoxy:
Straight or
Right Teaching

Ortho = Right

Doxa =
Teaching/
Doctrine

Orthopraxy:
Straight or
Right Living

Ortho = Right

Praxis =
Practice/Life

Doxology:
Praise, The
Worship of God

Doxo = Praise

Logos = Word

important. Through doctrine we know God, and as we know God, we love and serve and worship Him.

Orthodoxy leads to orthopraxy: right doctrine leads to right living. Orthodoxy also leads to doxology. Right doctrine leads to right and pure and true worship of God.

1. God

God is pure being. God is before and apart from anything else. (Exodus 3; Psalm 50: 1-2, 21-22; Isaiah 44, especially verses 6-8; Revelation 1:8)

God created and sustains all things. (Genesis 1; Nehemiah 9:6; Colossians 1:15-20)

God is Holy. (Isaiah 6:1-6; 1 Peter 1:14-16; Revelation 4:8-11)

God is Three Persons in One Substance, the Trinity: God the Father, God the Son, and God the Holy Spirit. (Matthew 3:13-17; 28:19; Acts 5:3-4; 1 Corinthians 8:5-6; Colossians 2:9)

As the doctrine of God is foundational to all other doctrines, it is important that we think biblically about God. One of the major themes of the Bible is the "Godness of God," that God is transcendent and majestic. When Scripture speaks of God as holy or of God's glory, it is referencing the Godness of God. Habakkuk says God's splendor is like the sunrise (Habakkuk 3:4), and Paul declares that God dwells in unapproachable light (1 Timothy 6:16). Below follows a confession of the doctrine of God. It stresses the Trinity by using groupings of threes. It attempts to provide a summary in a simple and even recitable manner

One Eternal God

We confess One Eternal God,
perfect and pure Being,
transcendent over all created things.

God is infinite, immutable, and impassible,
majestic in beauty, glory, and holiness.

God is spirit, without body;
God is simple, without parts;
God is sovereign, without rivals.

God is One Essence in Three Persons:
Father, Son, and Holy Spirit.

The Lord is God: abundant in
goodness, truth, and wisdom,

power, justice, and wrath,
mercy, grace, and love.

We love God above all else
for He first loved us.
We serve God in all things
for He made us for Himself.
We worship God alone
for He alone is worthy.

He was and is and shall be ever more.
Amen.

2. Bible

God has revealed Himself universally in nature, general revelation, and has revealed Himself specifically, special revelation. (Psalm 19; Romans 1:18-20)

The Bible is inspired by God and is therefore authoritative and inerrant. (Numbers 23:19; Proverbs 30:5; Matthew 5:17-18, 24:3; 2 Peter 1:16-21)

It is the direct revelation of God's will, and is to be obeyed. (Psalm 119; 1 Thessalonians 2:13; 2 Timothy 3:14-17)

How Do I Study the Bible?

As Christians, it is extremely important that we read God's Word. It is also important that we study it. Here are some basic tips.

1. Context is king. Always look at the context. Sometimes things that aren't clear become clearer to us as we keep reading.

2. Get help. God has given his church gifted pastors and teachers. Don't think that you have to learn everything on your own.

3. Have burning hearts. When Jesus met the disciples on the way to Emmaus he spent the journey pointing out all that the Old Testament had to say about him. When the disciples spoke of it to others they testified how their hearts burned within them (Luke 24:32). The Psalms speak of God's word as sweeter than honey. We need to read God's Word, study God's Word, and love God's Word.

4. Do it. James 1:22-25 reminds us of the importance of obeying God's Word and putting it into practice in our lives.

5. Pray. The Holy Spirit inspired the Bible and the Holy Spirit indwells all of us. He is our teacher (John 14:26).

3. Man

Man is created in the image of God. (Genesis 1:26-28; Genesis 9:6; James 3:9)

Man is both material and immaterial, or spiritual. (Genesis 2:5-7; Psalm 139:13-18; 1 Corinthians 15:42-58)

Man has dignity, and Scripture affirms the sanctity of human life. The Bible declares that humanity is both male and female, and sanctions marriage between man and a woman only. (Genesis 1:27; Genesis 2:22-25)

Since the fall of the first man, Adam, all mankind is fallen, alienated from God, and is under God's wrath. (Romans 5:12-21; 1 Corinthians 15:21-22; Ephesians 2)

The Old Testament uses a variety of Hebrew words and the New Testament uses a variety of Greek words to express both the depth and breadth of the atrocity of sin. (Psalm 51; Romans 3:9-20)

Who Am I?

There is a lot of confusion about who we are. We must look to what the Bible says about us. Here we learn ...

1. We are created in the image of God. We have dignity and every single person we meet has dignity.

2. We are fallen. This is true of every human being. We are all sinful.

3. In Christ, we are redeemed. Paul says we are "complete in Christ" (Colossians 2:10). If you have Christ, then you have all you will ever need.

4. In Christ, we are in community. We are members of Christ's body, of His church.

5. We are eternal beings. All human beings will spend eternity either with God or without God.

4. Jesus Christ

Jesus, the God-man, is the only mediator between God and man. (John 1:1-18; 1 Timothy 2:5-6; Hebrews 2:14-18)

Jesus accomplished redemption through His life, death on the cross, and resurrection. (Isaiah 53; Romans 3:21-26; 1 Corinthians 15:3-11)

Jesus is our Prophet, Priest, and King.

Prophet

The office of the prophet was established in the Old Testament. The prophet had two functions: to foretell and to forthtell. To foretell has to do with foretelling the future, with prophesying about the future. To forthtell is to proclaim God's will as declared in God's Word. Jesus foretold and he forthtold. He spoke with authority, declaring and revealing the Word of God. (Matthew 5:21; Matthew 24–25)

Priest

The office of the priest was also established in the Old Testament. The priest served the people of God as an intercessor. The priest carried out the sacrifices that were prescribed by God. The author of Hebrews declares Jesus to be our High Priest. Jesus is the priest who offered His own self as the sacrifice. Jesus is understood as our High Priest in two senses. First, he accomplished redemption through his atoning sacrifice. The Bible speaks of Jesus as having completed this work and as having sat down. The second sense of Jesus as our High Priest concerns His ongoing ministry of interceding for us before the throne room in heaven. In this role he stands as our High Priest. (John 10:11; Romans 8:34; Hebrews 2:14-18; Hebrews 7)

King

The office of king was also established in the Old Testament. The king represented God's people in a special way. The ideal king in the Ancient world was thought of as a brilliant counselor, a mighty warrior, a father-like figure, and, ultimately, as one who brings peace. All of these descriptions are attributed to Christ in the prophecy of Isaiah 9:6. (Psalm 110; Isaiah 9:6-7; Matthew 21:1-11; Revelation 19:11-16)

In the Old Testament, each of these offices were separate. Jesus is not only the perfect Prophet, Priest, and King, He is perfectly all three offices simultaneously. That leads the author of Hebrews to declare the absolute superiority of Jesus. (Hebrews 1)

The doctrine of the person and work of Christ is essential and central to the church. Without a biblical understanding of who Christ is and what He did, there is no proper understanding or preaching of the gospel. Without the preaching of the gospel there is no church. Below follows The Ligonier Statement on Christology, offering a summary of the doctrines of the person and work of Christ that draws from the creeds of the early church and the teaching of the Reformation.

The Ligonier Statement on Christology 2016

We confess the mystery and wonder
of God made flesh
and rejoice in our great salvation
through Jesus Christ our Lord.
With the Father and the Holy Spirit,

the Son created all things,
sustains all things,
and makes all things new.
Truly God, He became truly man,
two natures in one person.
He was born of the Virgin Mary
and lived among us.
Crucified, dead, and buried,
He rose on the third day,
ascended to heaven, and will come again
in glory and judgment.
For us, He kept the Law,
atoned for sin,
and satisfied God's wrath.
He took our filthy rags and gave us
His righteous robe.
He is our Prophet, Priest, and King,
building His church, interceding for us,
and reigning over all things.
Jesus Christ is Lord;
we praise His holy Name forever. Amen.

5. Holy Spirit

The Holy Spirit is personal, a being not a force. The Holy Spirit is God, the Third Person of the One Triune God. (Matthew 28:19-20, Acts 5:3-4; 1 Corinthians 2:10-11 and 12:4-6)

The Holy Spirit plays a unique role in the giving of life and in the giving of new life, the doctrine of regeneration, also known as the New Birth. (Genesis 1:2; John 3:1-8; Titus 3:4-7)

From the moment of the incarnation, the Holy Spirit played a crucial role in the earthly life of Jesus. (Luke 1:35 and 3:21-22 and 4:1 and 4:18)

The Holy Spirit played a unique role in inspiration, in revealing God's Word. (2 Peter 1:16-21)

The Holy Spirit convicts, regenerates, indwells, and seals, believers, guaranteeing redemption and the full inheritance of the riches that are ours in Christ Jesus. (John 16:7-11; Ephesians 1:11-14)

6. Salvation

Salvation is by grace alone, through faith alone, in Christ alone. (Habakkuk 2:2-4; Acts 4:8-12; Ephesians 1:3-14, 2:4-10)

The Puritan Thomas Watson once said that it takes two wings to get to heaven: the wing of repentance and the wing of faith. (Matthew 3:1-3; Luke 13:3; John 3:16; Acts 16:25-34)

Repentance means far more that feeling sorry for our sin. Repentance means seeing our sin as God sees it. Repentance involves a turning from sin. Faith involves a turning to God. The Reformers understood the biblical concept of faith as including three elements, using three Latin words: *notitia, assensus, fiducia.*

Notitia

This word means *knowledge*, bits of knowledge, like the English word notions. Biblical faith is about faith in propositions and pieces of knowledge. We could also call this the facts of the gospel. The facts of the gospel are these:

God is holy. I am not. There is nothing I can do that will remove or pay for my sins. Jesus is the only way. Through His life, His death, and His resurrection, He alone paid the acceptable and satisfactory price for my sins. (1 Corinthians 15:1-11)

Assensus

This Latin word means to assent. Biblical faith means assenting the facts of the gospel. One is saying, "The gospel is true." This is sometimes spoken of as head knowledge of the gospel. (John 20:24-29; 1 Thessalonians 1:9-10 and 2:13)

Fiducia

This means whole-personed trust. Not only does one mentally assent to the facts of the gospel, but one is wholly and unreservedly trusting in the gospel for salvation. (Romans 10:8-13; 1 John 5:6-15 and 5:20)

The gospel is both propositional and personal. The gospel is propositions, or statements of fact. The big three propositions are::

- God is just and holy and pure.
- All people are sinners and separated from God.
- Christ died on the cross for sin in order to bring people back to God

Salvation is also personal. We must believe that I am a sinner and that I am separated from God. And we must believe that Christ died *for me* and that He is *my* only hope of salvation.

Justification and Imputation

Two key words for the doctrine of salvation are *justification* and *imputation*. Justification means that we are declared righteous because of what Christ has done. Imputation is an accounting term. It means to apply to one's account. There is a double imputation. Our sins are imputed to Christ—they are accounted to him. Christ's righteousness is imputed to us—it is accounted to us. (Romans 5:1; 1 Corinthians 1:30-31; 2 Corinthians 5:21)

How Can I have Assurance of My Salvation?

One area that can be difficult for some is that of the assurance of salvation. Chapter 18 of the Westminster Confession of Faith offers a helpful treatment of this topic.

Westminster Confession of Faith, Chapter 18
Of the Assurance of Grace and Salvation

I. Although hypocrites and other unregenerate men may vainly deceive themselves with false hopes and carnal presumptions of being in the favor of God, and estate of salvation (which hope of theirs shall perish): yet such as truly believe in the Lord Jesus, and love Him in sincerity, endeavoring to walk in all good conscience before Him, may, in this life, be certainly assured that they are in the state of grace, and may rejoice in the hope of the glory of God, which hope shall never make them ashamed.

II. This certainty is not a bare conjectural and probable persuasion grounded upon a fallible hope; but an infallible assurance of faith founded upon the divine truth of the promises of salvation, the inward evidence of those graces unto which these promises are made, the testimony of the Spirit of adoption witnessing with our spirits that we are the children of God, which Spirit is the earnest of our inheritance, whereby we are sealed to the day of redemption.

III. This infallible assurance does not so belong to the essence of faith, but that a true believer may wait long, and conflict with many difficulties, before he be partaker of it: yet, being enabled by the Spirit to know the things which are freely given him of God, he may, without extraordinary revelation in the right use of ordinary means, attain thereunto. And therefore it is the duty of every one to give all diligence to make his calling and election sure, that thereby his heart may be enlarged in peace and joy in the Holy Ghost, in love and thankfulness to God, and in strength and cheerfulness in the duties of obedience, the proper fruits of this assurance; so far is it from inclining men to looseness.

IV. True believers may have the assurance of their salvation divers ways shaken, diminished, and intermitted; as, by negligence in preserving of it, by falling into some special sin which wounds the conscience and grieves the Spirit; by some sudden or vehement temptation, by God's withdrawing the light of His countenance, and suffering even such as fear Him to walk in darkness and to have no light: yet are they never so utterly destitute of that seed of God, and life of faith, that love of Christ and the brethren, that sincerity of heart, and conscience of duty, out of which, by the operation of the Spirit, this assurance may, in due time, be revived; and by the which, in the meantime, they are supported from utter despair.

7. Church

"No man is an island," said the poet John Donne. No Christian is an island, either. When we are saved, we become part of the body of Christ. (Romans 12:3-8; 1 Corinthians 12:12-27; Ephesians 2:19-22 and 4:1-16)

The Body of Christ is both invisible and visible, universal and local. What that means is this, all those who put their faith in Christ are part of the invisible church—the body of Christ, comprised of all believers of all time, from every corner of the globe. The church is also visible and local and made up of people in places. God has ordained the local church. (Acts 2:42-47 and 20:17-35; 1 Peter 5:1-5)

He has given two ordinances or sacraments to the church: The Lord's Supper and baptism. (Matthew 28:18-20; 1 Corinthians 11:17-24)

In the early centuries, church leaders spoke of "one, holy, catholic, apostolic church."

- One means a unified church around one Lord and one gospel.
- Holy means the church was made of believers, of genuine saints.
- Catholic means universal, not an ethnic or tribal people, but a truly universal church.
- Apostolic means committed to the teaching of the Apostles and grounded on the Word of God.

Since the time of the Reformation, we have the Protestant church and the many denominations. A true church is one that preaches the gospel and submits to the authority of God's Word and practices the Lord's Supper and baptism. (2 Timothy 4:1-5)

Different denominations disagree over how the Lord's Supper and baptism are to be administered. Denominations also disagree over church government, as well as over different understandings of doctrine. Despite these disagreements, the unity of the church is found in the one body of Christ, baptized by the one Holy Spirit, bound together by the one true gospel.

The Great Commission: Matthew 28:18-20

And Jesus came and said to them,

All authority in heaven and on earth has been given to me. Go therefore and make disciples of all nations, baptizing them in the name of the Father and of the Son and of the Holy Spirit, teaching them to observe all that I have commanded you. And behold, I am with you always, to the end of the age.

8. Angels, Satan, and Demons

In addition to the material and visible world, the Bible declares the reality of a spiritual and invisible world. The Bible speaks of angels and demons. (Genesis 3:24; Isaiah 6:1-7; Matthew 8:28-34; Revelation 20)

Angels played many roles in the pages of Scripture. The book of Hebrews tells us that angels are ministering spirits for the people of God. (Hebrews 1:13-14)

Peter warns us that Satan is a roaring lion seeking to devour us. (1 Peter 5:8-9)

We also see how Satan deploys demons in attempt to carry out his futile efforts. (1 Timothy 4:1)

9. Last Things

The Bible declares that Jesus is coming again. (John 14:1-4; Acts 1:6-11; Revelation 22:20). This is known as the Second Coming.

The Bible also speaks of a future judgement. Someday, the Book of Life will be opened. All those who belong to Jesus will spend eternity with the Triune God in the New Heaven and the New Earth. All those who reject Jesus will be condemned to eternal death in Hell. (Revelation 20:11-15 and 21:1-8 and 22:1-5)

10. Sanctification: The Doctrine of the Christian Life

How do we as Christians live now? This is called sanctification, or the doctrine of the Christian life. In Christ, we are new creatures. (Romans 6:5-11, 12:1-2; 2 Corinthians 5:17-21)

We live in and by the Holy Spirit. (Romans 8:1-17; Galatians 5:16-24)

Through the Spirit we are united to one another in the Body of Christ, the church universal. (Ephesians 2:18-22; 1 Corinthians 12:12-13)

We are called to be members of the local church. (Titus 1:5; Hebrews 10:24-25)

We are to love and serve God and our neighbor. (Matthew 22:34-40; James 1:22-27; 1 John 4:7-11)

We are to live for God's glory, knowing that we will spend eternity worshiping God in the New Heaven and the New Earth. (1 John 3:1-3; Revelation 21:5, 22:1-5)

THE CHURCH

After six days of creating, God rested on the seventh day. God is all-powerful. He is infinite in might. That means that God works at an infinite rate for infinity. He does not need to rest. So why does the Bible say God rested? God was establishing a pattern for His people to work and to rest. As we look at Genesis 2:1-3, we also see that God made the seventh day holy. The seventh day was set apart. In the Old Testament, this pattern became Sabbath worship as established by the second commandment of the Ten Commandments (Exodus 20:8-11). On the Sabbath, congregations gathered at the tabernacle or temple or in synagogues and worshiped together (Luke 4:16). When they gathered together they were devoted to reading and interpreting God's Word and to singing. The Psalms were the hymnal in Old Testament times.

The Sabbath came at the end of the week, day seven. Why the switch to Sunday, the first day of the week, as the day of worship? It is the day that Christ rose from the dead. The seventh day marked the end of God's work of creation. The resurrection, on the first day of the week, marks the end of God's work of redemption. We move from the seventh day to the first day, from Sabbath to Lord's Day.

We see this practice in the New Testament. In Acts 20:7, Paul is leading worship on the "first day of the week" in Troas. See also 1 Corinthians 16:2. In Revelation 1:10, John refers to Sunday as "the Lord's Day."

So much for the when of formal or corporate worship. What about the what?

The New Testament carries forward the Sabbath practices of reading and interpreting God's Word (preaching) and singing. Acts 2:42 identifies four things the early Christians were devoted to when they gathered together:

- The apostles' teaching
- Fellowship
- Breaking of bread (The Lord's Supper/Communion)
- Prayers

When Paul writes to Timothy and Titus in the Pastoral Epistles, he discusses the church offices and the requirements for officers, he stresses the need to teach sound doctrine, and he stresses the preaching of the Word.

Accordingly, the Reformers spoke of three marks of the true church:

1. The preaching of the Word.
2. The right practice of the sacraments or ordinances: Baptism and Communion.
3. Church discipline.

> "We can spare everything, except the Word."
>
> Martin Luther

One way we can understand the church is through the metaphors for the church used in the Bible. These metaphors paint vivid pictures of the role of the church in our lives and can help us understand more fully the nature and purpose of the church. They include the church as:

Flock	John 10:1-18, Acts 20:26-30
Building	1 Corinthians 3:11, Ephesians 2:18-22
House	1 Timothy 3:14-15, Hebrews 3:6
Temple	Psalm 118:22, 1 Peter 2:6-7
Body	Romans 12:4-6, 1 Corinthians 12:12-31, Ephesians 4:11-16
Bride	Ephesians 5:21-33, Revelation 19:6-9
Family	Ephesians 2:19

HYMNS

God's people sing. Worship through song has always been a key element in church life and in discipleship. Paul instructs us to address "one another in psalms and hymns and spiritual songs, singing and making melody to the Lord with your heart" (Ephesians 5:19). The church has a rich tradition of hymns that come from every century and from every corner of the globe.

One key moment of hymn writing came during the Reformation. Luther loved music. He wrote to Frederick the Wise, the prince of that region in Germany, the following lines on December 1523:

> Grace and peace. I am planning, according to the examples of the prophets and the ancient fathers, to create vernacular psalms, that is hymns, for the common folk so that the Word of God remain with the people also through singing. Therefore, we are looking everywhere for poets.

Luther was one of those poets, writing the classic Reformation hymn, "A Mighty Fortress Is Our God." It is full of doctrine and also full of emotion. It was written during a difficult year in the life of Luther. Luther based the hymn on Psalm 46. It may be the greatest hymn of all time.

"A Mighty Fortress is Our God," Martin Luther, 1529

A Mighty Fortress is Our God,
A Bulwark never failing;
Our Helper He amid the flood
Of mortal ills prevailing:
For still our ancient foe
Doth seek to work us woe;
His craft and power are great,
And, armed with cruel hate,
On Earth is not his equal.

Did we in our own
strength confide,
Our striving would be losing;
Were not the right Man on our side,
The Man of God's own choosing:
Dost ask who that may be?
Christ Jesus, it is He;
Lord Sabaoth His Name,
From age to age the same,
And He must win the Battle.

And though this World,
With devils filled,
Should threaten to undo us,
We will not fear,
For God hath willed
His Truth to triumph through us:
The Prince of Darkness grim,
We tremble not for him;
His rage we can endure,
For lo! his doom is sure,
One little Word shall fell him.

That word above all earthly powers,
No thanks to them, abideth;
The Spirit and the gifts are ours
Through Him who with us sideth:
Let goods and kindred go,
This mortal life also;
The body they may kill:
God's truth abideth still,
His Kingdom is forever.

Luther was the father of hymns for the German church. For the English church, we look to Isaac Watts. His hymns were first published in 1707. He wrote many, many hymns including "When I Survey the Wondrous Cross," "Our God, Our Help in Ages Past," and a great hymn we usually sing at Christmas, "Joy to the World." Watts was soon joined by others to write English hymns. John Newton wrote "Amazing Grace." The brothers John and Charles Wesley wrote somewhere around 6,000 hymns. That's amazing.

Back in Ephesians 5:19, Paul mentions hymns and spiritual songs. One such spiritual song from the modern age was first published in *Old Plantation Hymns* in 1899 and is entitled, "Were You There." It was likely written sometime in the nineteenth century. When we look at the Psalms we see Psalms of rejoicing and praise. There are also Psalms of lament. This spiritual represents that category of lament.

Were you there
when they
crucified my Lord?
Were you there?

Were you there
when they
crucified my Lord?

O sometimes
it causes me
to tremble!
tremble!
tremble!

Were you there
when they
crucified
my Lord?

Good hymns teach us good doctrine and assist us in worshipping God. They are a true gift to the church.

A sampling of some hymns you might want to look up include:

1. *"Our God, Our Help in Ages Past"*
   Isaac Watts, 1719

2. *"And Can It Be"*
   Charles Wesley, 1738

3. *"Come, Thou Fount of Every Blessing"*
   Robert Robinson, 1758

4. *"Amazing Grace"*
   John Newton, 1779

5. *"How Firm a Foundation"*
   Robert Keene/John Rippon, 1787

6. *"In Christ Alone"*
   Keith Getty/Stuart Townend, 2001

7. *"The Secret Place"*
   R.C. Sproul/Jeff Lippencott, 2015

Do you have any favorites you want to add to the list?

WORSHIP

When we sing hymns together we worship God together. We need to remember, however, that worship is far more than singing. Worship is the calling of our lives. Theology, or doctrine, is ultimately doxology. That means that the study of God, which is theology, ultimately leads us to worship God, which is doxology. Everything we do as Christians we are to do as worship. Our obedience is worship. Our service is worship. Our development and use of our gifts and talents is worship. The whole purpose of God creating us and redeeming us is so that we could worship Him.

When we get to the last book of the Bible and the heavens are peeled back for us to see what's happening, we find worship. Revelation Chapters 4 and 5 paint a beautiful portrait of all the grandeur and majesty of heaven and heavenly creatures worshipping God and bowing before His throne. All of history culminates in the worship of God. Culminate means it finds its purpose, like an arrow hitting the target or a soccer ball going to the back of the net. All of the actions of our individual lives ultimately culminate in the worship of God.

From the early centuries of the church, the people of God made doxology an essential and central feature of the church service. They didn't want to wait until they got to heaven to sing songs in worship of God. They wanted to worship God now. The *Gloria Patri* and the *Doxology* have been sung for many centuries by the people of God. Around the turn of the 1800s, Reginald Heber penned the hymn, "Holy, Holy, Holy." Read Revelation 4:8 and 4:11, as well as 5:9-14 and you'll find the words of the heavenly chorus. Think of those biblical passages and these hymns as you worship God.

The Gloria Patri

Glory be to the Father, and to the Son,
and to the Holy Ghost;
As it was in the beginning, is now,
and ever shall be: world without end. Amen.

The Doxology, 1674

Praise God from whom all Blessings flow,
Praise him all Creatures here below,
Praise him above, ye Heavenly Host.
Praise Father, Son, and Holy Ghost.

"Holy, Holy, Holy"

Holy, Holy, Holy! Lord God Almighty!
Early in the morning our song shall rise to Thee;

Holy, Holy, Holy! Merciful and Mighty!
God in Three Persons, blessed Trinity!

Holy, Holy, Holy! All the saints adore Thee,
Casting down their golden crowns around the glassy sea;
Cherubim and Seraphim falling down before Thee,
Which wert, and art, and evermore shalt be

Holy, Holy, Holy! though the darkness hide Thee,
Though the eye of sinful man, Thy glory may not see:
Only Thou art holy, there is none beside Thee,
Perfect in power in love, and purity

Holy, holy, holy! Lord God Almighty!
All thy works shall praise Thy name in earth, and sky,
    and sea;
Holy, Holy, Holy! merciful and mighty,
God in Three Persons, blessed Trinity!

As Christians we have the privilege of worshipping God, the Holy God who made all things and is making all things new. We were made to worship God. There's nothing greater we could possibly do. Someday we will worship God perfectly and in purity in heaven. For now, while we live on earth, worship is our calling and we have the great honor to do it every day.

For from Him and through Him and to Him
are all things.
To Him be the glory forever.
Amen.
(Romans 11:36)

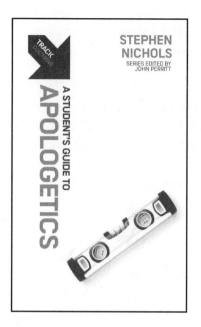

It's good to be prepared for hard questions. And if you're a Christian, hard questions are going to come. The Bible says we should be prepared to give an account of our faith, and so Stephen Nichols has written this short book to help you defend what you believe. Read, and make sure you're ready.

ISBN: 978-1-5271-0967-4

A.S.K.

REAL WORLD QUESTIONS / REAL WORD ANSWERS

DAVID ROBERTSON

We all have questions about Jesus, the Bible, the Christian faith and our culture today. The great news is that Jesus gives answers. These questions were gathered from teenagers in fifteen countries in five different continents.

These answers may lead to more questions which is fine – but the main aim of this book is to see and know better the One who is the Answer, Jesus Christ.

There are 52 short chapters. Each contains a question, a Bible passage, something to consider, recommended further reading and a prayer.

ISBN: 978-1-5271-0339-9

CHRISTIAN FOCUS PUBLICATIONS

Christian Focus | Christian Heritage | CF4K | Mentor

Christian Focus Publications publishes books for adults and children under its four main imprints: Christian Focus, CF4K, Mentor and Christian Heritage. Our books reflect our conviction that God's Word is reliable and Jesus is the way to know him, and live for ever with him.

Our children's publication list covers pre-school to early teens. We also publish personal and family devotional titles, biographies and inspirational stories that children will love.

From pre-school board books to teenage apologetics, we have it covered!

**Find us at our web page:
www.christianfocus.com**

CF4•K
*Because you're never
too young to know Jesus*